The Mommy Dot

J. M. Dazzles

Illustrator Toshio Yshikawa

Copyright © 2019 J. M. Dazzles
All rights reserved
First Edition

PAGE PUBLISHING, INC.
New York, NY

First originally published by Page Publishing, Inc. 2019

ISBN 978-1-68456-108-7 (Paperback)
ISBN 978-1-68456-109-4 (Digital)

Printed in the United States of America

I want to dedicate this book to my amazing son, Steven Alexander Melendez (Sam), for always supporting me and believing in The Mommy Dot. I want to thank Samantha, for helping me throughout this entire process, Robert, for pushing me to excel and Nena, for being my sister, my person! I love you!

I want to send a special shout out to Robbie and Michelle! This adventure started because of you!

Have you ever wondered how Mommies can tell when their kids are not telling the truth? Have you ever heard of "the Mommy Dot"? Well, let me tell you the story of how the Mommy Dot changed my life forever.

I am Sam, and when I was a little boy, I always had a "way with words" when trying to get out of trouble until I found out about the Mommy Dot.

It's 7:30 p.m. My tummy is full from the yummy dinner my mommy made for me. My teeth are brushed, and I am clean as a whistle.

Mommy whispers, "Sam, it's time for bed."

I walk to my room and sit up in bed.

Why do I have to go to sleep? I thought. *It is not fair that I have to go to sleep, and Mommy gets to stay up and watch TV.*

Mommy walks quietly into my room, tucks me in, lays down with me, and hums my favorite lullaby. She's not a great singer, you know, but I love it just the same. Usually, I fall fast asleep, but tonight is different.

Ugh! Why do I have to go to bed? I'm not even tired! I thought.

I pretend that I am asleep. Slowly and quietly, Mommy gets up from my bed and tiptoes out of my room. I peek through one eye. She's gone.

I tricked Mommy into believing that I was sleeping! I said to myself.

I gently pull the covers down and bit by bit roll off my bed. *Thump!*

"Oh, no! Did Mommy hear me?" I whispered.

Trying not to make a sound, I pull the door open with my tiny hands, stick my head out into the hallway and peer past the kitchen to the living room. I hear the TV on.

"Ugh! This is so not fair!" I said.

I slither like a snake on my belly toward the sound, moving from side to side, hoping that I am not spotted. Slowly, I make my way to the end of the hallway.

When I get to the end of the hallway, I see Mommy sitting on the couch in the living room. Mommy is watching TV and so am I. My mission is complete.

Suddenly, I hear Mommy's voice. "Sam, I hope that you are in your bed, sleeping!"

I freeze, and my eyes open wide. Quickly, I jump to my feet and tiptoe as fast as I can to my room.

Did I just get caught? I thought.

Tucked in my bed, eyes closed, I hear my mommy push my bedroom door open. I don't think I'm even breathing when she stands in front of my bed.

"Sam, were you out of bed?"

"No, Mommy, I wasn't!"

"Then what is that purple dot I see on your forehead?"

"What purple dot?" I bellowed in confusion.

I slap my forehead with the palm of my hand, and roll my eyes backward, trying to see the purple dot. I do not understand.

I run to the bathroom, flick on the lights, lift my hair up, and look in the mirror.

"There is no purple dot on my forehead!" I said loudly to myself.

"Mom! There's no purple dot on my forehead!" I exclaimed as I stood at the door of my bedroom.

"Sam, when children lie to their mommies, a dot appears on their forehead that only Mommies can see."

"Mommy, do all children get a purple Mommy Dot when they lie?" I ask, confused.

"I wouldn't know the color of their dot, Sam, because I can only see yours," she said.

Again, covering my forehead with my hands, I cry, "Mommy, I don't want that purple dot to stay there! Make it go away!"

"Don't cry, my sweet little boy, the purple dot is only there when you lie to Mommy. So let me ask you again. Sam? Were you out of bed?"

I fling my arms wide open and yell, "Yes! Yes! Yes! I was out of bed, Mommy! Is the purple dot gone now?"

"Yes, Sam, the Mommy Dot is gone. You told Mommy the truth, and the Mommy Dot is no longer there. Now, I hope you learned to always tell Mommy the truth. Let's get to bed and go to sleep. You have school in the morning."

"Mommy, can you sing to me?" I asked as I fought to keep my eyes open.

My mommy laid in bed and sang my favorite lullaby until we fell asleep.

So, there you have it! That is the story of how the Mommy Dot changed my life forever. It taught me to always tell the truth.

Until next time!

About the Author

J. M. Dazzles has been an educator for over twenty-six years. She is an avid reader and a dog lover. She is also a single mother, raising her son, Steven, in Miami as well as her three miniature schnauzers—Sookie, Phoebe, and Summer. Twenty-two years ago, when Steven was three, she decided to use the Mommy Dot as a way to teach him to tell the truth. Over the years, she shared this concept with friends and families, and they also used the Mommy Dot with their own children. Until the age of ten, she utilized the Mommy Dot with Steven. J. M. Dazzles decided that she wanted to share her experiences with the Mommy Dot with Mommies all over the world.

CPSIA information can be obtained
at www.ICGtesting.com
Printed in the USA
BVHW022035270919
559657BV00001B/1/P

9 781684 561087